Anna

Benjamin

Katherine

KATHERINE

Katherine's nightdress is based on a shift of coarse linen cross-stitched with initials at the top center front. Narrow ties gather in the extra fabric to form a ruffle from the flat fine linen flap extending above the neck casing; flat cuffs also of fine linen. Original initials on actual garment: A W; about 1800–1815. New England, private collection

BENJAMIN

Benjamin's white linen nightshirt is based on the common pattern for men's shirts of the period, in a slightly lengthened version. The longer length may indicate that this family can afford not only separate clothing for nightwear but also the expense of the additional fabric.

ANNA

Anna's married initials are cross-stitched at the top of her shift, which has a wide softly squared neckline. Stitching on original garment: P S 2; 1800–1815. Western Reserve Historical Society (85.12.9)

Other shifts of the period had small tapes or strings in the neckline hem to gather in the fullness. Women often embroidered numbers onto their personal garments as well as household linens to extend the life of the fabric by rotating the items numerically, assuring equal wear.

THE FOWLER FAMILY CELEBRATES STATEHOOD AND A WEDDING

An Illustrated History with Paper Dolls

Mary K. Inman and Louise F. Pence

Paper Dolls by Norma Lu Meehan

Texas Tech University Press

Introduction

In 1803, Ohio symbolized the American Dream. Although Ohio had just joined the Union, becoming the first state created from the Northwest Territory, it was sparsely populated and still considered to be part of the Western Frontier. Statehood, a simple fact of history to us, was the most exciting event in many of the young settlers' lives. Americans, young and old alike, talked of "Ohio Fever." Ohio was the epitome of all that many Americans hoped for—inexpensive, abundant land and the opportunity to better themselves. In addition, slavery had been prohibited by law. Those who stayed longer than the average five years, who worked hard, and upon whom Fortune smiled, were in fact able to achieve what became known in the twentieth century as the American Dream. These early settlers began by living in a survival mode with land to clear and shelter to build, but wholesome food was usually plentiful. **Game** was readily available, and crops such as corn grew rapidly in the rich soil. Families toiled together, and as others continued to arrive from the East, many prospered and began to accumulate some material goods. Families, symbolized here by the Fowlers, could better themselves by growing surplus crops to sell or trade, or by providing a needed service through such businesses as a general store or a **gristmill**. Nearly every family was willing to pay a miller to grind grain into flour.

Thus they moved beyond basic survival. Education was becoming a priority for many. Local newspapers were published and Eastern papers arrived regularly by U.S. Mail. The desire to improve their lives was a strong motivator; the settlers also believed deeply in the democratic philosophy that all men are created equal. This belief in equality translated into daily life. Activities such as quilting bees and barn raisings were attended by everyone—those with more and those with less. As these early settlers banded together to help each other, they combined socializing and work.

In this text, we have attempted to look at everyday life in early Ohio. Ordinary Americans of 1803 worked hard to obtain basic necessities. Although nineteenth-century standards of cleanliness did not include bathing, they did focus on clean clothing. This meant that individuals striving for refinement needed to change clothes and to launder them more frequently. The majority of the population lived on farms, often in isolated areas. Life for the ordinary person was physically exhausting; days were long and work filled. Disease and death were common events over which no one had any control. A religious revival (now called the Second Great Awakening) was sweeping the country, but the fervor seemed especially strong in the Western lands. The Methodist system of establishing regular circuits and of meeting in homes reached many on the frontier. This legacy lives on in most small towns where you will still find a Methodist church. The Baptists, Presbyterians, and Roman Catholics, among others, followed.

For the most part, Native Americans, the original inhabitants, were now living north and west of the **Greenville Treaty Line** (1795). To survive, they were forced to give up more and more of their lands. The Greenville Treaty Line was not respected by some white settlers, who felt that if no one was actually living on the land and farming it, the land should be available for ownership and settlement. Mohawk Chief Joseph Brant's philosophy of sharing the resources of the land, "one bowl, many spoons," did not work for people who interpreted ownership differently. The Native Americans and their farmer/hunter/gatherer lifestyle were being pushed continually westward.

Clothing of the frontier settlers of 1803 was as diverse as it was everywhere else in the country, depending on availability of materials, religion and cultural background, income, local customs, and general lifestyle. This was a time of great change. Clothing reflected major transitions occurring in the political, economic, and social arenas. Styles for both men and women had changed dramatically from that of the Revolutionary period. Americans followed styles in France and England, but had to adapt them to available materials and circumstances of their lives on the American frontier. Fabric was still usually hand produced, and purchased goods were difficult to obtain and expensive. Waistlines for both men and women were rising, but not everyone wanted or could afford to dress in the latest styles. For example, knee breeches were still acceptable for men, but the longer pantaloons reaching below the knee and tucking into boot tops became popular, as were those with tighter and longer legs reaching to the tops of the shoes. All of these styles were being worn until long pants (a later American idiom for pantaloons) became accepted dress for work and informal occasions. Some clothing terms became interchangeable or varied with geographic region. The word *vest*, for instance, was becoming synonymous with the older term *waistcoat*. Few examples or written primary sources referring to underwear

of the period survive. Women, especially those on the frontier, probably wore a variety of styles of **corsets**; some adapted from the fully boned **stays** of the eighteenth century and some looser and more comfortable to wear under the new softer, high-waisted dresses or for the hard work of daily life. Even many experts disagree. Hence, we discuss the possibilities and variety of underwear, but only illustrate women's shifts and men's shirts, the basic underwear of the period. Interest in classical Greece and Rome was responsible for changes in fashion as well as many other changes and trends. Among these were softly draped fabrics, a straight columnar look, flatter heels for women, and the popularity of wearing white.

Because we have highlighted one special day in the lives of the people of a small fictional community, our examples (selected from the 1800–1810 period unless otherwise noted) reflect only what individuals might have worn on such an occasion. Examples of clothing of the ordinary person from this period are difficult to locate because the valuable fabric was often worn out, remade to fit another person, or cut up for other uses such as quilts and rags. Moreover, because all paper was still made from linen or cotton, frugal families often sold their scraps and rags for cash. For this occasion, the hunting clothes, the linen or buckskin leggings and hunting shirt still favored by the settlers, along with many other popular styles, are not illustrated. Most of the articles of clothing are illustrated directly from, or are based on, items found in collections of ten North American museums and historical societies that generously supported the project. With few exceptions, the garments cited are located in Ohio.

To construct an accurate picture of ordinary dress in this early period from which so few unaltered pieces remain, we have also relied on travelers' journals, frontier diaries and memoirs, and newspapers, as well as a wealth of scholarship on clothing worn in the United States and England at that time. Our fictional characters, the paper dolls, are also created from these sources to achieve our goal of illustrating a variety of clothing styles that might have been worn in this time and place.

In July of 1803, Meriwether Lewis was still in Pittsburgh overseeing the keelboat construction for the forthcoming Lewis and Clark Expedition up the Missouri River and on to the Pacific Coast. It would be a matter of only a few years until the American frontier moved beyond the lands of the Old Northwest Territory, but Ohio remained a gateway to the West.

THE FOWLER FAMILY CELEBRATES STATEHOOD AND A WEDDING

An Illustrated History with Paper Dolls

Married—on Monday last, Mr. William Howe, to the amiable Miss Anna Fowler, both of this county.

July 7, 1803

Monday, July the Fourth, 1803: Fowlerton, State of Ohio

In the misty quiet of early morn, Katherine and Benjamin Fowler smile at each other and reminisce as they watch the sun rise over the hills beyond the languid East Fork. So much has happened in the fourteen years since they journeyed with their four children down the Ohio River to this fine new Ohio Country.

Life has been good to them, and they are grateful. They now have a **gristmill** and a new two-story log home. The mill has attracted new settlers, and the little crossroads town has become known as Fowlerton. Mother remembers the hardships of feeding the family mostly corn and **game** and of providing all their clothing. Father recalls the difficult task of cutting down the thick forest of trees and vines to plant his first corn crop and to build their crude log cabin. He and his elder son Josiah later built the gristmill on the edge of the East Fork of the Little Miami River.

The mill will be silent today. This is Independence Day, and everyone throughout America will be celebrating. This is one of the few holidays that all Americans celebrate. It will be a special holiday because Ohio has been a state only since the General Assembly convened on the first day of March 1803. There is also another event to celebrate: a wedding. Daughter Anna is getting married. Katherine and Benjamin comment on Anna's happiness since she met the schoolmaster William Howe. Anna suffered a deep loss several years ago when her **betrothed** died of **consumption**. For the past month, Katherine, Anna, and fifteen-year-old Martha have been busy sewing **linens** for Anna's home and clothes for her wedding. How fortunate that the family can now afford a new dress for each, as well as new shirts for Father and George, Martha's twin brother. Because time was short, Mother and Martha

have helped Anna piece a new sixteen-patch quilt top. The squares of hand-spun and hand-woven **wool** were cut from fabric scraps, which are never thrown away. The neighbors held a quilting **frolic** to quilt, or sew, the top, the wool filling, and the backing together. Last evening Anna completed the fine white linen wedding shirt she has hand sewn for William. Today, she and William will wed. Holidays are always a good time for a wedding because everyone plans to take a day off work, and the entire community will participate in the games and festivities.

Mother and father are concerned that Brother Jones, the Methodist circuit rider, may have met with an accident or illness. He has not yet arrived. On his previous visit four weeks ago, Brother Timothy Jones agreed to return for the wedding on July the Fourth. If he does not arrive today, who will officiate at the wedding? Must the wedding be postponed? There is unspoken hope among the family members that Brother Jones will arrive in time. Meanwhile, preparations are well under way for the forthcoming festivities.

Josiah, the eldest of the four Fowler siblings, is now a lieutenant in the **infantry.** He arrived yesterday, accompanied by Luke, a young noncommissioned officer. When the festivities are over, they will be on their way to Fort Knox near Vincennes. After dinner yesterday, the family listened to Josiah's and Luke's colorful descriptions of their new assignments in the Indiana Territory with its vast undeveloped lands. Josiah's military service has kept him away so long. Mother and Father are pleased that he has a special leave now that Fort Washington, located near Cincinnati, has been closed.

Mother and Father, still standing outside the front door, watch George walking toward the barn. He has grown to be tall and strong, helping Father at the mill since Josiah joined the U.S. Army in 1797. On his way

---

The form of the marriage announcement was taken from *The Western Spy and Hamilton Gazette,* Vol. 1, No. 6, July 2, 1799.

to feed the livestock and milk the cows, George wears the old linen shirt that he wore to bed as a nightshirt. He wears no other underwear, having tucked the long shirttails into his well-worn but cool tan-colored knee **breeches** of **tow linen** . He saves his only pair of **leather** shoes by wearing his center-stitched buckskin **moccasins**. They are comfortable, especially when worn with the thick natural-colored wool **stockings** knitted by Mother's own hands. His everyday sleeveless single-breasted **waistcoat** is made of **cotton**, which

Shirt for men

Mother dyed a soft butternut brown. Because the shirt is still considered to be underwear, the men all wear sleeveless waistcoats, even during the summer months and when doing chores. All of the boys and most of the men wear their hair cut short, at or above their ears, and the men are all clean shaven, in the current style. A few men still cling to the old ways, wearing long hair tied at the back of the neck in a **club**. The Fowler men and boys are fortunate that they can afford to barter with **country pay** for straw hats to wear during the hot summer months. Country pay is the common term for the exchange of goods without using money. The Fowlers often barter or trade with the grain they receive as a **toll** each time they grind grain for a local farmer. The Fowlers' mill exacts a standard toll of about one-eighth of the grain they grind.

This quiet time together before dressing for the day has been a special treat for Mother and Father. They are both still wearing their nightclothes. Last year Aunt Lizzie gave Mother her first long white linen nightdress. Her old muslin **nightcap** ties under her chin. Father's white linen nightshirt is also a recent luxury. It, too, is a slightly longer version of his day shirt. They consider themselves fortunate to have this special night clothing to wear only for sleeping.

As they turn in the doorway to reenter the house, the entire household is awakening. The young Fowler cousins, Caleb, Rachel, and David, the baby, their eyes still full with sleep, are already in the kitchen with

Martha. They have become cherished members of the Fowler household since their parents died this past spring of **dysentery**. Orphaned children in the early nineteenth century are commonly separated and adopted into different households because feeding even one extra person is difficult for most families. The three children are fortunate to be living all together with Aunt Katherine, Uncle Benjamin, and their cousins.

Martha has dressed Caleb, age four, in a dark print **frock**. At the back of his dress, she has tied the narrow **tapes** that have been threaded through **casings** at the neck and under the arms. The double casings on each sleeve gather in the fullness of the fabric as the **drawstrings** are tied. Hem tucks can be let out and drawstrings can be adjusted as he grows. Little boys wear dresses or frocks until they are **breech**ed into trousers or long pantaloons, usually between ages four and six. Later today, Caleb will wear his first long trousers. Rachel's short hair is still damp with curls after sleeping through the hot summer night. At six years old, she wears a simple frock made from the faded cotton print of Mother's former "**best dress.**" Tucks above the **skirt** and sleeve hems can be let out to make the garment longer and are also decorative. Martha carries six-month-old David on her hip. She has tied on a clean **nappy**, which is cool against his pale skin. Over his nappy she has tied on a dry flannel **pilcher**, which absorbs excess moisture. His white cotton cap and loose infant shirt with **cap sleeves**, which is pinned at the back, help to keep him comfortable on such a warm morning.

Martha moves about the **keeping room** with the knowledgeable assurance of a grown woman. She will take Anna's place helping Mother with all the food preparation. Anna will be running her own household after she marries later today. Martha's **short gown**, worn over a cotton **shift** and soft **corset**, is made of a brown cotton print, which complements her fair complexion. The dark yellow-gold **linen** of her petticoat is soft with wear and many washings. It covers her underpetticoat of natural linen. Martha wiggles her toes against the rough texture of the **puncheon** floor and smiles to herself. She is going barefoot this morning as she often does in warm weather. Her white cotton **kerchief** around her neck and shoulders is damp from the heat of the hearth and the warm summer morning. Her ear-length, light brown hair curls about her neck and face, resembling the styles in the latest fashion plates from the East.

Mother moves quickly through the cooking area into the **bedchamber** she shares with Father. She smiles as she steps out of her nightdress to put on her shift, remembering that not so long ago she had only the shift to wear both to bed and during the day. She pulls on her white cotton stockings and ties them with dark blue tape **garters**, in the older style, just above the knees, before slipping on her old black buckled shoes. Katherine's **stays**, now called a *corset* by many women of the time, lace in the back. The corset is shorter than stays of the past. Mother ties on **pockets** that she embroidered with bright-colored flowers several years ago. Her outer petticoat of blue-and-white striped homemade linen has side slits for easy access to her pockets. The red print cotton short gown ties at the center front with narrow tapes threaded through casings at the neck and high above the waist. It is loose enough to be cool on this hot summer day. Mother puts on her blue-and-white checked linen **apron** above her natural waistline and ties it in the back. She also wears a fine white **lawn** kerchief every day instead of the homemade linen one she used to wear. Since the mill is doing well, she is able to afford a finer fabric for her kerchiefs. Mother is still partial to covering her head with the old style **mob cap** when working about the house.

Father has finished dressing in his work clothes. Mother made his white linen shirt, which comes almost to his knees. Men's shirts have changed little these past many years. Separate pieces of fabric sewn along the shoulder line and **gusset**s under the arms reinforce the seams and make this shirt more durable. For working, he leaves off the white linen **neckcloth**. He has also begun wearing, as underwear, linen **drawers** under his breeches or **pantaloons**. They are constructed with separate legs attached to a waistband with roominess in the seat to allow ease of movement. The drawers extend to just below the knees. Having withstood several years of hard use, Father's **work-a-day** buckskin breeches also extend below his knees and fasten with buttons and self-ties. The **front fall** fastens to the waistband with buttons. The waistband can be adjusted in the back with ties and an inserted gusset. He wears white cotton stockings with his moccasins, which protect his feet and allow him to save wear and tear on his boots. Father buttons his dark **indigo**-blue linen summer waistcoat as he hurries out to the barn to help George.

Anna is sitting quietly near the table, cross-stitching initials on William's new fine linen shirt. She wants to have it finished before the men come up to the house for breakfast so that William can wear it for the wedding. Anna awakened at daybreak in her cotton shift. She dressed quickly for the morning with a clean shift under her best dress of pink linen printed with flowers. Father selected the fabric for this dress on one of his trips to Cincinnati more than a year ago. She wears no separate corset with this dress as its **bodice** lining overlaps tightly across the front and is pinned. Narrow tape ties threaded through casings at the

Shift, showing body & sleeve gussets

rounded neckline fasten the top of the print dress. The skirt is sewn to the high waistband with **stroked gathers** for fullness. She has worn her white linen apron for so long that it feels as comfortable as an old friend. For the sake of comfort, and to save precious shoe leather, Anna is barefoot on this fine July morning. The heat and humidity of July has encouraged the curliness of Anna's hair. She has short fringe around her face, with longer ringlets in the back, which she pulls into a **Grecian style** mass of curls.

The unmarried men and the boys arrive at the house for breakfast and will eat first. Because of the expense, Mother had waited a long time for the set of six matching locally made chairs, one for each adult in the family to use at the old long table. Having company means that the family must eat in shifts, the men usually served first by the women of the household. The men have spent the night a short distance away at the original Fowler cabin where Anna grew up. Normally, travelers would expect to sleep on the floor of the house or in the log barn. Josiah was pleased when William, having put the finishing touches on the new glass windows, invited all to stay in the cabin that he and Anna have been fixing up to be their home. Anna's easy-to-make **whole cloth quilts** are always useful. Frontier women make them by sewing together lengths of hand-woven wool for both the top and underside. Linen thread quilts the warm fluffy wool filling between the two layers. Anna's best quilt of purchased printed cottons is both **pieced** and **appliquéd.** William has moved his clothes and books from the house of the neighbor with whom he has been **boarding**. In these early years, nearly everyone lives at home, helping their parents until they marry and set up their own household. Individuals like William, living away from home, pay room and board to stay with a family. This arrangement also helps the family, as they receive payment in cash, goods, or labor.

When Benjamin built the new log house, he offered the original one-room cabin as a temporary schoolhouse for the small community. Using the trees cut today, the men of the village will raise a separate log

whole-cloth quilt

building to serve as schoolhouse and village meeting house. Tonight the original cabin with its loft and massive hearth will again be home to a family.

At the table, Josiah and Luke join the other men already seated. George has milked and fed the livestock. Father has helped by straining the milk through a piece of linen into a clean wooden bucket before bringing it into the house. Josiah and Luke are prepared to help out where needed. Luke, recently promoted to the rank of sergeant, is wearing the standard-issue **coarse linen** work clothes of the enlisted men. The white **frock** (sometimes called a smock) is full and to the knees. The frock is constructed like a large shirt and is worn over long **fatigue trousers** of the same fabric. The trouser legs come to the tops of his black leather shoes. Luke's hat is simple, black, and round, with a fairly narrow brim. A bearskin crest or strip of fur decorates the **crown** from back to front and helps to deflect rain from the wool felt. The white deer-tail plume, the white string looping that attaches the leather **cockade** to the crown, and the pewter eagle stand out impressively against the rich black of the wool and bearskin hat. Although the eagle is part of the military uniform because it is a symbol of the young United States, it is commonly used as a decoration throughout America.

Josiah proudly wears his short white linen **vest** or waistcoat with a band collar over his standard-issue white linen shirt. At the collar of his shirt, he wears a stiff black silk **stock**, which fastens at the back of his neck. (Luke, as an enlisted man, is issued a black leather stock.) Josiah's white linen pantaloons, with a blue stripe down each outside seam, fit tightly. His black **Hessian boot**s with tassels are common wear for all commissioned officers. Because of the informality of the family breakfast, Josiah has not put on the wool coat he will wear later in the morning.

As William enters the house, Anna smiles and hesitantly hands him her gift, the wedding shirt. He is surprised and warmly appreciative, telling everyone how proud he is of Anna and of her sewing skills. He takes his place at the table. William wears his finest for his wedding day. His white linen summer pantaloons are tucked into his shiny black Hessians. Of course he will

change into his new shirt before the wedding. His yellow-and-white, horizontally striped wool waistcoat is a strong contrast to his coat. Because of the warmth of the **keeping room**, he removes his new white linen coat (similar to a man's suit jacket or sport coat of today), with long squared tails. He purchased his new black **beaver hat** of the latest style with a narrow brim and high flat **crown** in Cincinnati.

Mother and Anna set the food on the table while Martha watches her three young cousins. The men pull up their chairs and begin to eat their breakfast of corn cakes, bread, milk, coffee, and, as a special treat, butter and honey. Because of the guests today, this meal is much more elaborate than the Fowlers' usual corn cakes and cider or milk.

Anna is the first to notice the commotion of an approaching rider in the yard outside the front door. She runs out to greet Brother Timothy Jones as he wearily dismounts. He has been on horseback since very early morn. Last week, he explains, he had been taken with the **ague**, as malaria was called in eighteenth and nineteenth centuries. He spent several days in bed with the alternating fever and chills from which many settlers of the Ohio Valley suffer. But he has made up for lost time, and all is well. He removes his broad-brimmed black hat as he enters the Fowler home. The circuit rider joins the other men at the table gratefully, for he is still somewhat weak and weary after his many hours on the road. Since he recently married a widow with several children, he has applied to his bishop to become a local preacher and to settle with his new family near Fowlerton. Everyone here is accustomed to Brother Jones's simple, somber, and somewhat out-of-fashion clothes. His white linen shirt is frayed at the cuffs. His collar, like that of the other men, is secured under his chin by a neckcloth, wrapped around the turned-up collar. The center of his neckcloth is placed at the front. Its ends wrap completely around his neck and tie in a knot (or bow) in the front. He is fortunate that his wife found enough black wool cloth to make a long coat and breeches of the same fabric. He wears a dark-brown glazed wool single-breasted waistcoat made with the longer skirts of the older style. In his pockets, he carries three small books—the Bible, a hymnal, and the Book of Discipline. His skillfully mended white cotton stockings and buckled shoes make him seem a little old-fashioned and more formal.

Like many men of the sparsely settled countryside, they do not talk at the table, but attend steadfastly and urgently to the business of eating. There is still work to do before returning to the cabin to finish dressing.

As the men quickly depart, Anna and Mother clear the table of the **trenchers**, reminders of their first years of settlement. Now it is time for the women to break their fast. Mother asks Martha and Rachel to set the table with the knives, three-pronged forks, and silver teaspoons, as well as the imported English **cremeware** (she calls it queensware) plates that Benjamin bought her last year. English potteries ship untold thousands of cremeware items to America every year. Katherine is using her best tableware for the meal to be shared with the other women. For this day, Katherine has invited her widowed sister Lizzie and Sarah, Anna's girlhood friend, who moved with her family from Fowlerton to Cincinnati several years ago. Aunt Lizzie will be coming to live with the Fowler family to help Mother. She is dressed in a new grey-green **silk** dress, a welcome change from the black **mourning** clothes she has worn for the last year, since she buried her beloved husband. Her dress has long straight sleeves, a low neckline, and the popular **apron front** high

wooden and silver spoons

waist. The decorative tuck above the hemline adds body and weight to the bottom of the skirt. Aunt Lizzie wears a white ruffled **chemisette** under her dress to fill in the neck of the bodice. It has no sleeves and is secured by ties under each arm. Her large oval mourning **brooch** is pinned at the center front of the neckline. The mourning brooch has a delicately plaited inset of her late husband's hair under the oval glass dome. Her mourning ring contains the hair of her only child who died in a hunting accident. Aunt Lizzie's fashionable silk **turban** covers her hair, leaving a fringe of curls about her face. Over her arm she carries a long, rectangular, creme-colored wool shawl that in the evening will ward off the chill. Woven geometric shapes of blue, green, and red edge the length of the shawl. Larger forms of the same pattern and fashionable fringe finish the ends.

Anna's girlhood friend Sarah has traveled from Cincinnati, where she lives with her married sister. An

Ladies turban examples

accomplished seamstress, Sarah has sewn her own fine white cotton lawn dress made in the very latest fashion. Its low neck and high waist are very flattering for Sarah. The short sleeves are trimmed with more fabric and a tassel. Over her shift and under her pale **underdress**, Sarah wears a band of fabric rather than stays. She wears the new **pantaloons,** a fashionable type of underwear for women. They look like loose linen tubes on a waistband. She wears white silk stockings and white leather slippers with thin **slip heels**.

Sarah and Lizzie have been staying with a neighboring family and have just now arrived for the unusually late breakfast. As this is a special occasion, Mother will serve some of her imported tea, still a precious commodity in this frontier area. She steeps the tea leaves in her **pewter** teapot and pours it into tea cups with deep saucers.

It is late morning. Breakfast is finished and the dishes washed. Mother is anxious for everyone to dress for the wedding. Mother and Aunt Lizzie will dress in Mother and Father's bedchamber. The children and the other women start upstairs to dress in the upper bedchamber normally used by the girls of the family. Mother reminisces about her own wedding as she dresses for that of her elder daughter. Aunt Lizzie smiles as she recalls Katherine and Benjamin's simple wedding, held just before Benjamin joined General Washington's troops.

Mother tightens her corset a bit and slips on her blue cotton print dress. She was able to buy this fabric, along with some of the other **yard goods** needed for the new clothes, using **hanks** of linen thread that she had spun and dyed as country pay. The long sleeves of her dress fall straight from small puffs at the shoulder and end just below the wrist. Drawstrings tie at the center front at the neckline, but the dress fastens at the back with tape ties threaded through fabric casings at the neck and waist. The narrow self-fabric ties secure the high-waisted look that is so fashionable. Mother's best cotton stockings have blue **clocking**. She feels very elegant as she slips on aqua pigskin slippers with slip heels that she bought in Cincinnati. Mother touches up her hair, which has been curled and pulled together high on her head so that the curls fall softly.

Upstairs there is happy confusion as the younger women dress for the wedding. Martha, at age fifteen, feels very grown up as she dresses in her new clothes. She pulls her linen **chemise** over her head. It has short tight sleeves and is much less full than her old one. Her white underdress is a kind of lining for the dress and falls gently to just above her ankles. Martha pins together the linen under bodice of her new, fine white cotton dress made just like Aunt Lizzie's. Like the other women wearing the high-waisted dresses, she ties a small pillow or padded roll at the inside back waist to preserve the vertical line of the garment. Martha slips her pink flat slippers over her new cotton stockings. She fluffs her short light brown hair with her fingers.

Martha then turns her attention to the children. She dresses Rachel in a cotton chemise with short sleeves. Over Rachel's head, she pulls a white cotton, high-waisted, short-sleeved dress. Then, over the dress she places a blue print apron or **pinafore** that ties at the back. Mother has cut and sewn Rachel's cotton stockings as well as her white linen flat slippers. Martha, however, sympathetically sets aside Rachel's shoes and stockings because of the heat of the day.

Next Martha turns to Caleb. Although **skeleton**

shoe examples: one with ties; one with buckle

suits are popular for little boys in well-to-do families, Caleb had asked for trousers and a vest to look like George's and Uncle Benjamin's. Mother was able to make over Josiah's and Father's **hand-me-downs** to fit Caleb. The ruffled collar of his linen shirt is like that of other young boys. The front fall of his dark blue linen trousers fastens with flat metal buttons. Martha buttons on Caleb's vest, made from scraps left over from Benjamin's waistcoat. The back is made of cheaper brown linen with two sets of tape ties for adjusting. Mother has found for Caleb the homemade red tie shoes with buff trim that George had worn as a child. Caleb is so excited that he dances a little jig.

Martha picks up the baby David. Over his nappy and shift, she pins on a long petticoat and then his gown. At six months, he is almost too old for such a long dress. As soon as he begins to crawl and stand up, he will need to be in short frocks. The long gown he wears today is of fine cotton mull, with a short bodice, long gathered skirt, and puffed sleeves. The gown is trimmed with white embroidery of wheat and the Grecian key design. Clothing and decoration in the style of the ancient Greek or Roman patterns are very popular.

Anna shrieks with delight as she opens Sarah's gift. Sarah has sewn her a simple but fashionable white dress, much like Martha's, of fine cotton. She has also sewn two cotton print long-sleeved spencers, one green and one pink, to wear over the dress in cooler

weather. Spencers are short jackets, usually with sleeves, worn over the fashionable white dresses. Anna is thrilled now that she will have two dresses for special occasions!

Sarah and Martha prepare to help Anna with her new brown silk wedding dress. Anna runs her fingers over the beautiful silk, a gift from her soon-to-be husband. William had asked his mother to send the fine silk fabric from Boston. Her eyes fill with happy tears as she thinks about spending the rest of her life with such a thoughtful, kind, and loving man.

Over her chemise, Anna puts on short stays. She then pulls on her new silk apron front dress and ties the softly squared silk neckline at the front. Long sleeves extend just beyond her wrists. The skirt is gathered over the bodice hem at the high waist by the brown tapes drawn through the front casing and tied in the back. Today, for the wedding, Anna will wear a gold-colored silk bonnet and carry a **reticule,** a fashionable small handbag. She uses these same accessories for all special occasions. After the wedding, this will become Anna's best outfit.

Meanwhile, at the cabin, George, who at age fifteen often works as hard and as long as any man, joins the other men as they dress. Luke is changing into his summer dress or parade uniform. He secures the collar of his standard white linen shirt with a high black leather stock, fastening it at the back with its brass clasp. The long shirt tucks into his white linen overalls, which close with a front fall that buttons at the waist. A narrow blue stripe sewn at each outside seam contrasts strikingly with the white linen. His overalls are made without **tongues** so they do not fasten under the shoes. His black **gaiters**, which button over the bottom of his overalls, like boot tops, fasten under his black shoes to give his uniform a crisp appearance. He then slips into his nine-button sleeveless, collarless white linen vest.

As they dress, Luke explains to George that the facings and skirt **turnbacks** of military coats are of a different color from the coat itself. In early times, men going into battle would turn up their cuffs, turn back the front opening, and pin up the skirts of their coats to make it easier to fight. In time, the different colors of the lining became the contrasting colors of decorative front facings, cuffs, and turnbacks. Luke's cutaway military coat is of dark blue wool with red collar and front facings and white turnbacks on the long coat tails. Pewter buttons stamped with the number of his regiment trim his coat. He talks proudly about his army issue clothes that are made by tailors. As an enlisted man, he receives each year a new supply of clothing, which includes such items as a coarse linen frock and fatigue trousers for work details; a coat of cloth; vest and waist-length jacket of linen; overalls of

attach to sides
of cap

Hearth; its size accomodates preparation of several dishes at the same time by use of hot coals and several small fires. Iron cranes and S hooks also allow the cook to raise and lower cooking temperatures manually. Typically, a family accumulates additional cooking utinsels (e.g., gridiron, toaster, spider, kettles and pots of various sizes, tin reflecting oven, etc.) throughout the years.

KATHERINE'S SHIFT

Woman's shift is made with squared neckline, cut and hemmed to create a front "flap". 1780–1810. Western Reserve Historical Society (58.223). [The flap might have concealed the corset top.]

White knit stockings are common and popular for all women, although colored stockings can also be worn.

MARTHA'S WHITE COTTON KERCHIEF

MARTHA IN SHORT GOWN AND PETTICOATS WITH THREE CHILDREN

Short gowns are still worn over the shift, stays, pockets, and petticoats for work. This cotton print short gown is worn over several petticoats with slits at side seams to give access to separate pockets. Under petticoat of natural linen; outer petticoat of finer linen dyed soft gold. Simple white apron is gathered on a waistband.

BABY DAVID

Infant shirt of soft cotton; ruffled cap sleeves; squared neckline with flap; no date. Ross County Historical Society (1947.165.05)

Infant cap of fine cotton; fine tapes and casings; sewn with pulled-work trim; no date. Ross County Historical Society (1959.98.03)

CALEB

Boy's brown linen print frock; tape through casings at sleeves, neckline, and high waist; hem tucks permit lengthening; about 1808–1811. Massillon Museum (BC 400.14.3)

RACHEL

Simple child's frock, or dress, based on popular style of the day; made from fabric of Mother's old dress.

Women's nightcaps usually tie under the chin, while day caps, when worn, often set on top of the hair.

Windsor chair; style produced widely throughout United States; those made in Pittsburgh readily available in Ohio.

Le Moyne Star quilt; pieced blocks of small-patterned dress cottons and bordered with larger-print furnishing chintz; decorative appliques from other furnishing chintz on yellow blocks; about 1800–1825. Ohio Historical Society (H21420)

Katherine in short gown and petticoat

Over the chemise or shift, women still wear stays, sometimes called a corset. Pockets attached to a woven tape tied on over the stays. Petticoats tie on over the stays and pockets. Side slits near waist to access the pockets are hidden by the "skirts" of the red cotton print short gown. The popular blue-and-white checked homespun linen is gathered onto a waistband with stroked gathers, creating a full apron. Frontier women still fancy blue, white, and red as favorite colors.

George's waistcoat

Short, butternut-brown cotton waistcoat or vest; straight pockets; buttons covered in dark brown cloth; 2"-wide band collar; natural linen lining. Unusual as vest back is also of heavy cotton fabric rather than cheaper linen. 1800–1820. Ohio Historical Society (H56997)

Men continue to wear waistcoats at all times, as shirts are still considered to be underwear in the early nineteenth century.

Benjamin's work clothes

White linen man's shirt; reinforcing fabric strip across shoulder; single button on shaped collar and at each cuff, as well as on neck placket; 1800–1850. Ohio Historical Society (H76441)

Indigo-blue linen waistcoat with band collar. Based on brown cotton waistcoat. About 1800–1820. Ohio Historical Society (H56997)

Buckskin breeches button at the front fall and button and tie below the knee; leather ties adjust the back gusset; buttons at waist are for braces; about 1809. Western Reserve Historical Society (50.356)

Anna's Pink Dress

White linen fabric printed with pink background; dark pink, yellow, and red floral pattern; fullness of the skirt is gathered at the waistband with stroked gathers. Rounded neckline ties at center front; high waistband fastens with hook-and-eye closure. Linen underbodice crosses and pins closed. Slits in side seams allow access to pockets. Gift of Reuben R. Springer, by exchange, 1797–1805. Cincinnati Art Museum (1986.993)

Anna's clean white apron is a sign of refinement.

Katherine's fine cotton kerchief

White hand-knit cotton stockings; knee length; 1800–1850. Ohio Historical Society (H76562)

Moccasins are still being worn on the frontier. Drawers or a pants lining are being worn at this time by more American men. The shirt is still considered the basic article of underwear.

Powder Horn

Pennsylvania
rifle

Benj

Jos.

Geo.

PENNSYLVANIA RIFLE

Father's best clothes

Long buff-colored nankeen
pantaloons or trousers; front
fall fastens with metal buttons;
about 1811. Western Reserve
Historical Society (61.77.1)

Red, beige, and brown cotton-
print waistcoat or vest; brown
linen back adjusts by tape ties;
fabric based on boy's print
waistcoat; about 1810.
Western Reserve Historical
Society (71.110.33)

Pantaloons tuck into brown
and black leather boots, with
woven pull-on loops or
bootstraps showing. About
1800. Western Reserve
Historical Society (54.221)

Adding a fine linen neckcloth
to the linen shirt and a blue
wool cutaway coat, Father is
dressed for a fine occasion
in Fowlerton.

POWDER HORN

Josiah's uniform waistcoat and trousers

Josiah's white linen waistcoat
or vest made in the popular
double-breasted style with a
high collar. White linen
pantaloons or overalls,
accented with blue stripes;
legs tuck into black Hessians
piped in red.

George's wedding clothes

Long white linen trousers;
front-fall closing with
bone-colored buttons.
Based on young man's
white linen trousers.
About 1800–1850.
Western Reserve
Historical Society
(40.1272)

Blue print waistcoat, worn
over white linen shirt
finished at shaped collar
with neckcloth. Black
wool coat, cutaway style
with long tails, is worn
year round. Black shoes
tied at the instep are
widely worn, and white
stockings are still popular.

Wide brimmed wool felt hat keeps out the weather during his travels.

Colonel Miller and Mrs. Miller

Off-white wool man's waistcoat or vest, decorated with silver tambour lace (made of finely silver-plated thread) embroidered onto the wool with pink or red thread and silver sequins; waistcoat back made of white linen. This vest belonged to General Arthur St. Clair, governor of the Northwest Territory (1788–1802) and former president of the Continental Congress. About 1785.
Fort Ligonier (79.28.16-18)

Man's fine linen shirt; ruffle at neck opening; collar 4½" high. (Illustrated neckcloth is typical, not original.) About 1750. Historic Costume and Textiles Collection, OSU (1988.318.2)

Ivory silk knee breeches and matching coat in the style of late eighteenth century.

Buckled shoes and clocked white silk stockings.

Woman's open robe of ivory satin. The boned bodice closes in the front by lacing cords through holes created in the linen lining; decorative tabs extend below the waistline. Covered buttons and silver sequins embellish the cuffs of the straight sleeves. A second pair of sleeves, narrow and wrist length, exist, but were never worn. Matching petticoat is stiffened and weighted at the hem with scalloped horsehair facing. About 1790.
Fort Ligonier (79.28.19–22)

Ivory satin shoes lined with linen; leather soles with pointed toes and 2 ¾" leather heels. Silver sequined trim matches that on dress cuffs and man's waistcoat. Made in Philadelphia. Shoes and open robe and petticoat belonged to Mrs. Arthur St. Clair. About 1770–1780.
Fort Ligonier (79.28.6 & 7)

White silk stockings with white clocking are still stylish.

Timothy Jones

This brown glazed wool waistcoat, worn over the standard linen shirt with neckcloth, is lined with brown linen; vest back is also of brown wool; black fabric covered buttons; collarless neckline; vest "skirts" extend below the waistline; 1785–1800. Ohio Historical Society (H21615)

Cotton-lined, black wool breeches. Glazed wool lines the pockets and the narrow front fall. Breeches fasten at the knee with five self-covered buttons. 1800–1825. Ohio Historical Society (H21610)

The dense wool coat fastens at midchest with two hooks; decorative buttonholes. Based on Thomas Worthington's wedding coat; the original is of light blue or grey, with mother-of-pearl buttons; 1796. Ohio Historical Society (H86021)

Hand-knit cotton stockings.

Buckled shoes: still preferred by some men, although both "tie" shoes and boots are being worn.

The hymnal (book of religious songs) is small so as to fit in his coat pocket (located in the "skirt" of his long coat tails).

Fowler Family Log House

Circuit Rider Timothy Jones

Colonel and Mrs. Miller

Aunt Lizzie

Mourning Brooch and ring

Sarah

Luke

COPPER FRAMED, OVAL SHAPED MOURNING BROOCH

Glass covers the plaited hair; fastens as a pin or worn as a pendant using small ring at one end of oval. Inscribed: T.B. 1797. Gift of Mr. and Mrs. Charles Fleischmann. 1797. Cincinnati Art Museum (1999.262)

Copper mourning ring containing plaited hair covered with glass. Can be sized by the use of three holes and one pin on the back of the band. Inscribed: "Lewis Deblois Ob:9.Feb. 1799 AE.71". Gift of Mr. and Mrs. Charles Fleischmann in memory of Julius Fleischmann.1799. Cincinnati Art Museum (1991.68)

SARAH

Fine white cotton dress; narrow casings for tapes that tie in the back at

neck and high waist. Elaborate white embroidery on bodice and hem, tassel trim on sleeve back. 1800–1810. The Historic Costume and Textiles Collection at The Ohio State University (1988.318.127)

Flat, slip-heeled leather slippers. Based on aqua-blue slippers, 1800–1810. Fort Ligonier (79.28.8 &9)

Women's gloves are a sign of refinement. Long gloves, extending above the elbow, are usually worn with short-sleeved dresses.

Reticule of dark creme-colored satin.

LUKE

Luke wears the basic standard issue infantry summer uniform of white linen. The short linen waistcoat is worn over a linen shirt, the collar held up at the neck with a black leather stock. The long linen overalls or pantaloons are accented by a blue fabric stripe. Black gaiters extend from midcalf to fasten under black shoes.

AUNT LIZZIE

The grey-green dress of thin silk ties at the center neck and waist back; high waist with apron front skirt; tuck above hem to add body. (Worn for a wedding at Adena, near Chillicothe, Ohio); 1800–1810. Ohio Historical Society (H5006)

A plain, cream-colored wool shawl (25 ½" by 108 ½"); red, blue, and green geometric pattern woven into fabric trims the ends and sides of the fabric; decorative fringe completes the trim. Worn by Mrs. Edward Tiffin, wife of Ohio's first governor. About 1812. Ross County Historical Society (1989.83.502)

Flat leather slippers with pointed toes and slip heel. Based on blue slippers, 1800–1810. Fort Ligonier (79.28.8 &9)

Chemisette: fine white cotton "underblouse"; widely used to fill in the neckline for modesty.

Martha's Wedding Clothes

Short-sleeved linen chemise and long white underdress form a "lining" under the finely woven, white-on-white, striped cotton dress; ties at neck front; apron-style front skirt wraps around waist and ties at back. Based on grey-green silk dress, about 1800–1810. Ohio Historical Society (H5006)

Pink cotton stockings with pink flat slippers. Based on blue slippers, 1800–1810. Fort Ligonier (79.28.8 & 9)

Short white leather gloves would complete a stylish look.

Pewter Teapot; oval; wood handle. About 1762–1820. Ohio Historical Society (H35299)

Teacups; typical fine teacups with deep saucers.

Black Felted Men's Hat

Bonnet or hat made of gold silk woven in a flower and wheat pattern. Knitted cotton lace lines and trims the brim. [Ribbons under chin replaced on actual item.] About 1800–1820. Ohio Historical Society (H59009)

Anna's Brown Silk Wedding Dress

Brown silk, apron-front dress; bodice lined with natural linen; front linen underbodice fastens by two flaps that cross over to pin closed; long sleeves are set far into the narrow back; 1/2 inch tuck above hem; 1800–1815. American Textile History Museum (1100.2.11)

Brown leather slippers bound and trimmed with pale blue leather; pointed toes and flat slip heels; tie at "open flap" across instep; about 1790–1800. Western Reserve Historical Society (62.82.3)

Short leather gloves [white or soft tan would be proper for this occasion].

The reticule illustrated here matches the silk of the hat. [It would be common for a reticule not to match any part of a woman's attire.]

Anna's Heart-in-Hand Ring

The heart-in-hand ring was becoming more popular in America as a betrothal or wedding ring.

William Howe

The yellow-and-white wool waistcoat, worn over a white linen shirt with neckcloth, has ribbed horizontal stripes, metal buttons, a high band collar, and straight welt pockets. Israel Putnam III wedding vest, 1795. Ohio Historical Society (H18942)

White linen pantaloons are tucked into stylish Hessians for summer wear. Based on buckskin breeches, about 1809. Western Reserve Historical Society (50.356)

The white linen cutaway coat and black hat complete the groom's wedding attire.

William

Anna

Martha

Caleb   David   Rachel

Cremeware
(queensware); off-white
glazed earthenware first
produced by Josiah
Wedgewood; copied by
many potteries.
Transferware plate in
popular Willow pattern.

ANNA'S PINK SPENCER

Spencer made of pink, yellow,
and red vine-print cotton; thick
pink satin braided trim at
neckline; about 1805. Western
Reserve Historical
Society (55.126)

Porcelain teapot; raised
lavender Minerva pattern;
Chelsea, English; about
1745–1784. Ohio Historical
Society (H35133)

ANNA'S GREEN SPENCER

Spencer of green, yellow, and
ivory cotton print; oval
neckline outlined with braided
green satin trim; about 1805.
Western Reserve Historical
Society (55.127)

KATHERINE'S DRESS FOR WEDDING

Dress of small geometric print on cotton; a self-fabric tie threads
through a flat fabric casing to tie at back. The short upper sleeves
are gathered to fit onto the straight lower sleeve. Two rows of tucks
near the hem; slight train would be taken up by the small pillow-
like bustle tied inside the waist back. About 1800–1810. Ohio
Historical Society, Educational Collection

Pigskin flat slippers, dyed aqua blue, are lined with linen; leather
soles with pointed toes and slip heels; 1800–1810.
Fort Ligonier (79.28.8 & 9)

RACHEL

Rachel's simple white cotton dress is typical for young girls of the
time; full skirt, gathered onto a short plain bodice with short
sleeves. Most girls wear colored pinafores or full aprons to protect
their dresses. (Based on two watercolors of sisters Sarah Ann
Worthington (H86202) and Mary Tiffin Worthington (H84256) who
lived at Adena. About 1808–1811. Ohio Historical Society

CALEB

Boy's vest or waistcoat; small geometric brown-and-red print on
white cotton; vest back of brown linen; lined with white linen;
about 1810. Western Reserve Historical Society (71.110.33)

Boy's trousers of blue linen close with a front fall fastened with flat
metal buttons; about 1812. Western Reserve
Historical Society (42.4712)

Child's shoes; red fabric uppers sewn onto leather soles;
topstitching and eyelets of tan thread; tan ribbon binds and trims
the uppers; about 1790. Western Reserve Historical Society (42.683)

White linen shirt with open ruffled collar typical for little boys of
the period, as are white cotton stockings.

BABY DAVID

Long infant dress of fine cotton mull; high, embroidered bodice;
long skirt embellished with Greek Key design and wheat pattern;
about 1800–1810. Kent State University Museum (1983.1.54)

ANNA'S WEDDING GIFT
FROM SARAH

Soft white cotton dress,
typical of the period, has
narrow casings at neck,
long sleeves, and
highwaisted apron front.
Waist tapes can cross in the
back and tie in the front, or
simply tie at the back.
Based on grey-green silk
dress, 1800–1810. Ohio
Historical Society (H5006)

Bearskin roach; deer-tail plume and black leather cockade

LUKE'S BLUE WOOL INFANTRY JACKET

Red facings, cuffs, and collar; closes at midchest with hooks; white turnbacks. Red wool epaulet on right shoulder indicates the rank of sergeant; white cross belt can hold a bayonet at his left side.

JOSIAH'S FULL UNIFORM, CROSS BELT, AND BICORN

A black silk stock at the neck and officer's cutaway coat of blue wool is added to the vest and pantaloons or overalls; red collar, facings, and cuffs trimmed with silver "lace" or braid; buttonholes also trimmed with silver lace; white turnbacks; front hooks together at midchest; silver epaulet on left shoulder indicates rank of lieutenant. As an alternative to the lace-trimmed coat, Josiah can also have his officer's coat made like that of the enlisted men, but of finer cloth and without the lace.

Sword belt with oval belt plate that serves as a buckle

Cartridge box; leather

MILITARY MUSKET

Military cockade; leather with pewter eagle; found at Ft. Mackinac; dated 1802. Mackinac State Historic Parks (1995.1.363)

Wool felt bicorn; worn by infantry officers

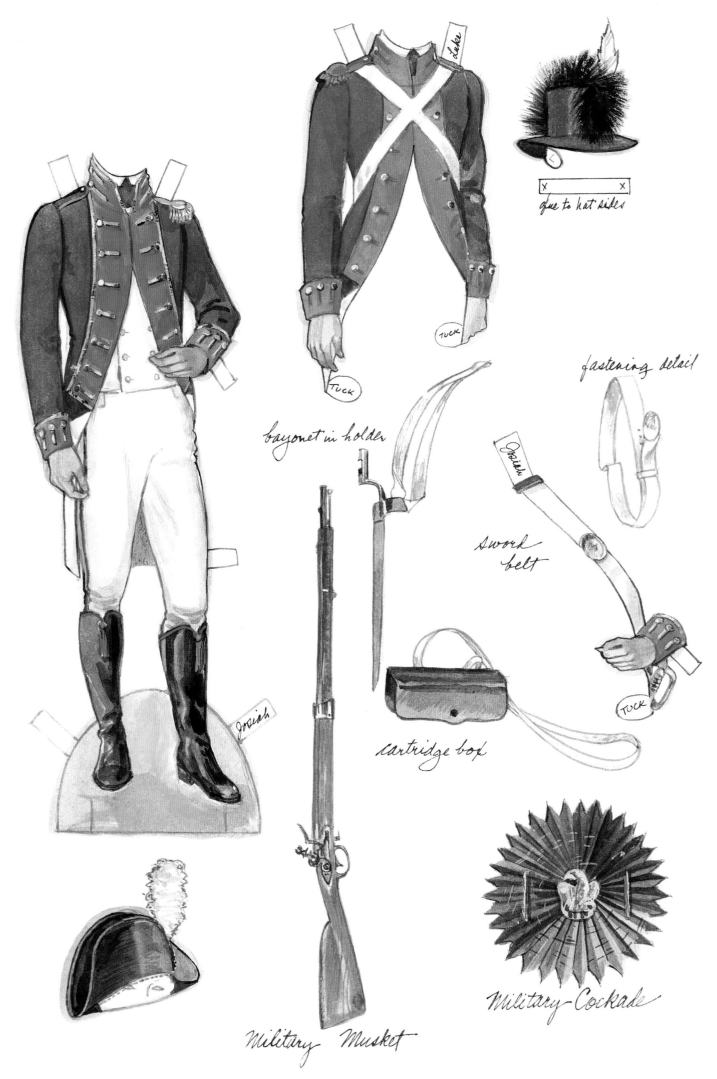

glue to hat sides

fastening detail

bayonet in holder

sword belt

cartridge box

Military Musket

Military Cockade

wool for winter and of linen for summer; and four shirts of linen. He even receives a new pair of gaiters and several pairs of socks.

While donning his dress uniform, Josiah answers George's questions about army life. The entire United States Army in 1803 consists of just over three thousand men—two infantry regiments and one regiment of artillery. American military policy relies primarily on state militias made up of volunteers. The regular army remains small. Professional soldiers in the regular army, like Josiah and Luke, are assigned mostly to the frontiers. Because Fort Washington has been abandoned, Josiah and Luke have been reassigned to the Indiana Territory where William Henry Harrison is the territorial governor.

Josiah wears his white linen summer **overalls** tucked into the tops of his tasseled black Hessians. Over his shirt, silk stock, and vest, he adds his blue cutaway coat with its white skirt lining. The red collar, cuffs, and facings are trimmed with infantry officer's silver "**lace**" or braid. Josiah's single silver **epaulet**, worn on his left shoulder, shows his rank as a lieutenant. Silver indicates that he is a member of the infantry. (Artillery officers' coats have gold-colored metal buttons and lace with a gold epaulet). In contrast, Luke's red **worsted** epaulet worn on his right shoulder indicates his rank as a sergeant. Josiah next tries on his **bicorn** hat for George. The large round brim is shaped so that the opposite sides meet at the top above the middle of the crown. The bicorn, a dress hat for all infantry officers, is decorated on the left side with a tall white plume held in place by a black cockade with a pewter eagle at its center. George is impressed at the snappy style with which Josiah can remove his hat to carry it under his arm. Over his shoulder and across his chest, Josiah fastens his white sword belt.

George has been so busy listening to Josiah and Luke that he must hurriedly change his own clothes. His new white linen pantaloons fit loosely, covering his white cotton stockings and extending to the tops of his one pair of shoes, made of black leather. He, too, has a new linen shirt sewn by Mother. He pulls up his collar and clumsily attempts to tie his neckcloth to look like Father's. Josiah helps with the neckcloth before George buttons his blue linen print waistcoat. He has decided to wait for the wedding to put on his black wool jacket made like William's. At last George feels that he looks presentable.

Father, too, has joined the men to change clothes. Mother purchased a very fine white linen fabric to make his new shirt and matching neckcloth. He is proud of his buff-colored **nankeen** pantaloons with flat metal buttons at the waist. As he pulls on his black leather boots by the attached bootstraps, he carefully

tucks in the fabric of each pantaloon leg. To hold up the long pantaloons so that the shirt will not show beneath the short fitted vest, he buttons on braces made with wide straps woven of wool and linen. His brown cotton-print waistcoat was the inspiration for Caleb's little vest. Father thinks that the fitted blue wool coat with a high collar, wide lapels, and long coat tails looks stylish enough to wear in any big city. The print of the waistcoat shows fashionably below the high cut of the coat. Now that the men have all finished dressing, they pack their gear and carry it up to the log house. They will stow it in an upper bedchamber until they depart.

As Mother inspects the children in their good clothes, she glances up with relief to see that the last guests have arrived. Their old friends, Colonel Miller and his wife, have come from Cincinnati. The Colonel is still addressed by his military title, although he has not seen military service these twenty years. The Colonel and his wife are wearing their most treasured garments, the very same clothes that they wore for festive evenings years ago. Because fabric is valuable, most good clothing is still altered to meet with fashion changes or is made over into a garment for someone else. It is not unusual, however, for some older persons to cling to the styles of their youth and to wear a best dress or suit for many years, even if it is no longer the style. The day is warm, but the Colonel wears his ivory silk breeches with a fine ruffled linen shirt and neckcloth. His matching coat, which he carries over his arm, is in the style of nearly fifteen years ago. His one concession to frontier life is wearing sturdy black buckled shoes rather than the matching silk dancing slippers he once wore. His single-breasted waistcoat is of a fine pale ivory woolen cloth, the bottom edge cut straight, but unlike Benjamin's vest, resting well below his natural waistline. The two-inch standup or band collar, the pocket tabs, and the waistcoat front are embroidered with silver thread and sequins to look like little flowers. These small shiny circles may look out of place on a July afternoon in 1803, Ohio, but they once sparkled in the candlelight of many a grand ball.

Mrs. Miller, known to all as The Colonel's Wife, is wearing an **open robe** of soft ivory satin. The dress is called an open robe because the skirt is open at the front to show her satin **petticoat**. Made of fabric similar to the Colonel's jacket and breeches, it has the same silver sequins sewn about the sleeve cuffs. Her precious **satin** dress is somewhat protected from perspiration by her washable cotton shift. Like most other women in America, she wears no other underwear. Over her shift, her stays have been laced tightly in the back to enable her to fit into the bodice of the dress. Because it is such a warm day, she tied on only two petticoats—still considered to be part of a woman's outer garments. Her first petticoat, or under petticoat, is made of cotton and linen. The outer petticoat matches her dress. Both have slits in the side to give her access to her pockets beneath. The dress itself fastens by a tape threaded through the hidden openings on both sides of the bodice front. She tucked a sheer white silk **fichu** into the bodice for modesty. Her white silk stockings, clocked in white, are held up by garters tied above her knees. The silver sequins scattered on the pointed toes of her matching silk heels still sparkle. The large ruffles of her cap frame her face softly. The Colonel and Mrs. Miller are welcomed warmly by old friends so pleased to see them again.

Jovially, the Colonel makes his way through the gathering outside the Fowler house. Brother Jones stands in the doorway. Anna and William, surrounded by family and friends, stand before him. All are silent.

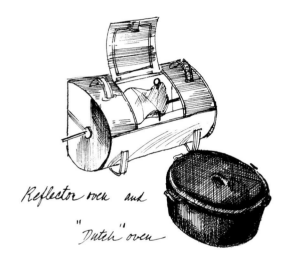

Reflector oven and "Dutch" oven

The preacher begins to read, and the wedding commences.

After the preaching, a roar erupts from the gathering and everyone attempts to congratulate the new husband and wife. The women press around the bride to exclaim over the **heart-in-hand ring** William has given to Anna. Wedding rings are not yet worn on the frontier by many wives (mourning rings are actually more common). Anna wears her ring on the index finger of her right hand. All rings, including wedding rings, are worn on whatever finger of whichever hand they might fit. The thumb and index fingers are both popular ring fingers.

Next to the house is a table that has been carried outside and adorned with Aunt Lizzie's iced cake containing candied fruit baked by Aunt Lizzie. In this relatively isolated town, on what is still considered the frontier, many people have never seen such a sight. Cider and shrub, a fruit drink made of crushed fruit,

sugar, vinegar, and water are set out for the thirsty guests. The Circuit Rider preaches temperance, so many guests drink the corn whiskey in moderation. It is often consumed in place of water that might be contaminated. Several other tables, made of slab wood set out near the house between tree stumps, are laden with food contributed by every household in the community. Among the dishes are small tea cakes (similar to modern cookies), pies of every description, preserves, and a variety of pickled foods, as well as meat of all types, especially game: venison, duck roasted in a tin reflecting oven, roasted passenger pigeons, and even bear. Corn pudding is also a favorite, along with cornbread and corn cakes. With so many people to feed, there is no concern for plates or eating utensils: all present eat with their fingers.

The afternoon's celebration continues after the midday meal with games, races, and contests of strength, especially for the men and boys. The women enjoy a rare chance simply to sit and socialize. Luke and Martha appear to have found much to talk about as they sit on a large tree stump. Josiah and Sarah, having not seen each other for nearly eight years, become reacquainted as they walk about the grounds. Father has been placed in charge of the felling of seventeen trees, symbolizing that Ohio, the first state created from the Northwest Territory, has proudly become the seventeenth state to join the Union.*

The men return to the house for more refreshment. Before the fiddle music for the dancing begins, all must drink a final toast to the Union. The Colonel, as the ranking officer, having served in the War for Independence, lifts his glass of cider to toast America:

> *To the Union: may the*
> *AMERICAN EAGLE soar*
> *triumphant when*
> *change approaches.***

---

*The felling of the seventeen trees on a Fourth of July actually occurred in at least one Ohio town, as recorded in the village of Worthington, July 4, 1804.

**The toast given by Colonel Miller is taken from the fifteenth of fifteen toasts made at the July Fourth Celebration, Cincinnati, Ohio, 1799. Recorded in the Cincinnati weekly, *The Western Spy and Hamilton Gazette*, Vol. 1, No. 7, July 9, 1799.

Glossary

ague   A fever usually related to malaria and identified by regularly returning chills.

appliqué   One fabric sewn on top of another for decorative purposes.

apron   A protective covering worn over the front of clothing.

apron front   A dress style in which the front of the skirt portion pulls up and ties over the bodice hem at the high waist like an apron; ties attached to the skirt front can be tied in the back or crossed in the back and tied in the front; the bodice and the skirt are sewn together only at the back.

beaver hat   Hat originally made with felted beaver hairs; by the early nineteenth century, the beaver population was nearly depleted and "true" beaver hats were very expensive. By 1803 these affordable top hats were made of felted sheep's wool, but probably included small amounts of other animal hair.

bedchamber   Bedroom or sleeping room.

bedgown   A woman's loose over-blouse worn for work along with a petticoat; similar to a short gown.

best dress   The one dress reserved by most women to be worn on special occasions; a garment not worn when working.

betrothed   Person one has promised to marry.

bicorn   A large round-brimmed hat shaped so that the opposite sides meet at the top above the middle of the crown.

boarding   Paying for food and lodging in a private home.

bodice   The top part of a dress.

breech   (verb, to breech) To put breeches or pants on.

breeches   Men's pants that fastened just below the knee.

brooch   Any large pin worn as a piece of jewelry.

cap sleeves   A very short sleeve that just covers the shoulder.

casing   A tape or narrow fabric hem sewn into a garment to form a kind of tunnel; tape, ribbon or string can be threaded through it.

chemise   In nineteenth-century America, a woman's shift. See **shift**.

chemisette   A high collared cotton or linen garment worn under a dress for modesty or warmth.

circuit rider   A preacher who travels a regular route from place to place to preach.

clocking   Fancy stitching used to decorate stockings.

club   Man's hairstyle; tied at back of neck and turned under.

coarse linen   See **tow linen**.

coat   Man's outer garment like a suit or sport jacket of today.

cockade   A badge-like decoration for a military hat, made of silk or leather.

consumption   A disease we call tuberculosis today.

corset   A stiff garment worn over the shift to hold the body straight and small.

cotton   The soft fibers from the boll of the cotton plant that can be spun into thread and woven into absorbent fabric of various weights.

country pay   A kind of bartering or exchange of homemade or homegrown goods for items from a store.

cremeware   Off-white, glazed earthenware first produced by Josiah Wedgewood; copied by many potteries; also called queensware.

crown   Top part of a hat above the brim.

drawers   In the late eighteenth and early nineteenth century, a man's undergarment for the lower part of the body. In 1803 still not commonly worn by American men.

drawstring   A string or tape pulled through a casing (hem) to gather in fabric.

dysentery   An illness characterized by diarrhea; often fatal in these early years.

epaulet   A shoulder ornament for military uniforms, usually indicating rank.

fashion plates   Engraving or drawings of the latest fashions often found on the frontier just weeks after their arrival on the East Coast from Europe.

fatigue trousers   Long pants to be worn by soldiers when they are doing heavy work.

felt   A nonwoven fabric made of wool, or wool and fur or hair, matted and pressed together to form a thick fabric.

fichu   See **kerchief**.

frock   (1) A man's loose outer garment, worn out like a large shirt.
(2) A dress; also a garment worn by little boys before they wear pants.

frolic   A party; sometimes included activities such as a quilting frolic (bee) or barn raising which included both work and fun.

front fall   A center front panel of men's breeches or pantaloons that buttons on each side at the waist to form a front closing.

furnishing chintz   Glazed or unglazed cotton print fabric; commonly used for drapes and upholstery.

gaiters   Leg coverings that go from below the knee to foot.

game   Wild animals hunted for food.

garters   Ribbon, tape or leather tied around the tops of stockings to hold them up.

Grecian style   Any fashion or design reflecting classical Greece and its artifacts.

Greenville Treaty   Treaty signed in August, 1795, following the Battle of Fallen Timbers, which among other terms established all land north and west of the treaty line as Indian territory forever.

gristmill   A building containing large mill stones for grinding or milling grains such as corn, wheat, rye, and barley.

gusset   A piece of fabric sewn into a garment seam to allow movement and lessen the strain on the seam.

half-gown   A dress that ends just between the waist and the knee; an everyday dress worn over a petticoat. See **short gown**.

hand-me-downs   Clothing or other personal items that have been worn or used by someone else, usually in the same family.

hanks   Coiled or looped standard lengths of yarn or thread.

heart-in-hand ring   A ring designed with clasped hands around a heart; such rings were known as far back as Roman times when they were related to making a contract.

Hessian boots   High boots usually with a tassel in the front; also called Hessians; named after the German troops who fought in the War of Independence.

indigo   A blue dye made from **indigo plants**.

indigo plants   Bushy plant used to make a blue dye. The leaves are boiled down to make a paste, hardened into large lumps, and then cut into cubes of indigo dye to sell. To dye cloth, the indigo must be added to an alkaline solution (in the 1970s urine was often used) because the dye is not water-soluble. After being soaked in this solution, the fabric turns blue upon its removal from the dye bath and its exposure to oxygen.

infantry   Foot soldiers.

keeping room   A common room in which the family cooks, eats, and lives.

kerchief   A large scarf made or folded into a triangle, worn around the neck over a woman's gown; could be tied, pinned, or tucked into the bodice; also called a fichu.

lace   On military uniforms, silver or gold braid.

lawn   A very fine, thin cloth made of linen or cotton.

leather   Tanned animal skin with the hair removed.

linen   Cloth made from the flax plant.

linens   (1) Household articles made of linen or cotton such as sheets and towels.
(2) Items of personal clothing such as undergarments, shirts and shifts, made of linen or cotton.

mob cap   White, gathered cap worn over a woman's hair.

moccasins   Slipper-type foot coverings made of animal skins; sole and upper are a single piece.

mourning brooch   A pin worn in remembrance of a loved one, often made with the hair of the deceased.

mourning ring   A ring worn in remembrance of a loved one, often made with the hair of the deceased.

mourning   Period of grieving following the death of a loved one.

mull   Soft, thin muslin.

nankeen   Yellow buff-colored heavy cotton cloth.

nappy   A diaper.

neckcloth   Men's neckwear, also called a cravat; a piece of fabric wound around the neck and secured or tied at the front.

nightcap   Traditional head coverings worn by men and women for sleeping.

open robe   A dress style usually called an open robe and petticoat; the skirt is open in the front to show the petticoat; petticoat need not match open robe.

overalls   Military pantaloons with tongues, which extended over the tops of the shoes and fastened like gaiters; could also refer to long pants without tongues.

pantaloons   (1) Man's long leg coverings, tighter than trousers. At this time the pantaloon length could vary from mid-calf to ankle.
(2) Woman's underwear consisting of two tubes of linen or cotton fabric attached to a waistband; not yet typically worn by the average American woman of this time period.

petticoat   A separate skirt-like part of a woman's clothing, usually showing beneath the short gown or open robe; can be used as an outergarment or an undergarment.

pewter   Silver-colored metal used for making buttons as well as tableware; cheaper than silver.

pieced   Small pieces of fabric sewn together.

pilcher   An English term for a diaper cover, often made of wool flannel, to help absorb moisture.

pinafore   A sleeveless apron-like garment worn by little girls.

pocket   A pouch attached to a tape and tied at a woman's waist, often worn in pairs under the petticoats. At this time pockets were not sewn into women's clothing.

puncheon   Roughly split logs laid side by side so that the flat surfaces would form a floor.

quilt   To sew together a soft filling between two layers of fabric; usually in an ornamental design.

reticule   A small handbag, made of fabric and held by draw-strings. The reticule was used to carry items that women formerly carried in their pockets. Pockets were too bulky under the new straighter silhouette.

satin   A silk fabric that is woven to produce a soft, smooth and glossy finish.

shift   A loose dress-like undergarment worn by women; also called a **chemise**; made of cotton or linen.

short gown   Top part of a woman's clothing extending over the hips and worn over a petticoat for work and informal occasions; also called a **bedgown** or **half-gown**; also spelled shortgown.

silk   Fabric made of the thread from the cocoon of silk worms; could be heavy and stiff or fine and soft.

skeleton suit   A two-piece suit that buttons together at the waist; worn by little boys in the late eighteenth and early nineteenth century.

skirt   Any part of a garment that hangs below the waist.

slip heel   A thin piece of leather placed between the sole of a shoe at the heel and the upper, to form a very slight elevation on a women's flat shoes or slippers.

stays   A woman's stiff garment that laced up tightly over the shift; also called a corset in the nineteenth century.

stock   Part of a military uniform; wide stiffened band of silk or leather worn over the collar; buckled or tied in the back; three inches high.

stockings   Long, thin socks usually extending over the knee; also called *hose*.

stroked gathers   Small pleat-like gathers.

tape   A woven strip of linen, cotton, or wool, often made by children on special small looms.

toll   A portion of the grain kept by the miller as payment for grinding the grain; about one-eighth, but varied by the kind of grain.

tongues   The part of men's overalls that extended down and over the top of the shoe like gaiters; only winter military uniforms were made with tongues.

tow linen   Very low quality linen made of the short or broken fibers of the flax plant; also called toe linen.

trenchers   Wooden platters or plates on which food was served.

turban   A head covering made by winding a long strip of fabric around the head.

turnbacks   That part of a military coat in which the skirt is turned back to show the lining.

underdress   A seperate garment that functions as a slip or lining and goes beneath a sheer dress and over the shift.

vest   Another word for **waistcoat**.

waistcoat   A man's upper garment that buttoned over the shirt; in the early nineteenth century, varying in length, usually sleeveless, and worn on all occasions.

whole cloth quilt   Lengths of hand-spun and hand-woven wool sewn together at selvages with thick wool filling and quilted. [Example illustrated in text is quilted in a block pattern; about 1813. Ohio Historical Society (H6571)]

wool   Soft wavy or curly undercoats of sheep or goats, the fibers of which can be spun into yarn and knitted into garments or woven into absorbent fabric.

work-a-day   Everyday, as in everyday clothes for work.

worsted   Woolen yarn or cloth.

yard goods   Fabric sold by the yard.

Bibliography

Appleby, Joyce. *Inheriting the Revolution: The First Generation of Americans*. Cambridge, MA: Harvard University Press, 2000.

Arnold, Janet. *Patterns of Fashion 1: Englishwomen's Dresses & Their Construction, c. 1660–1860*. New York: Drama Book Publishers, 1964,1972.

———. *A Handbook of Costume*. New York: S. G. Phillips, 1971.

Ashelford, Jane. *The Art of Dress: Clothes and Society 1500–1914*. London: The National Trust, 1996.

Baclawski, Karen. *The Guide to Historic Costume*. New York: Drama Book Publishers, 1995.

Ball, Robert W. D. *Springfield Armory: Shoulder Weapons 1795–1968*. Norfolk, VA: Antique Trader Books, 1997.

Bartlett, Virginia K. *Keeping House: Women's Lives In Western Pennsylvania 1790–1850*. Pittsburgh: Historical Society of Western Pennsylvania & University of Pittsburgh Press, 1994.

Bassett, Lynne Zacek. *Textiles For Clothing of the Early Republic, 1800–1850, A Workbook of Swatches and Information*. Arlington, VA: Q Graphics Production Company, 2001.

Baumgarten, Linda. "Altered Historical Clothing," *Dress: The Annual Journal of the Costume Society of America*. Vol. 25, 1998, 42–57.

Better Homes and Gardens Heritage Cookbook. Des Moines, IA: Meredith Corporation, 1974.

Bradfield, Nancy. *Costume In Detail: Women's Dress 1730–1930*. Second edition, 1981. [Originally published in England, 1968] New York: Costume and Fashion Press, 1977.

Buck, Anne. *Clothes and the Child: A Handbook of Children's Dress in England, 1500–1900*. New York: Holmes & Meier, 1996.

Burnston, Sharon Ann. *Fitting and Proper: 18th Century Clothing from the Collection of the Chester County Historical Society*. Texarkana, TX: Scurlock Publishing Co., 1998.

Burstein, Andrew. *America's Jubilee: How in 1826 a Generation Remembered Fifty Years of Independence*. New York: Alfred A. Knopf, 2000.

Byrde, Penelope. *Nineteenth Century Fashion*. London: B.T. Batsford Ltd., 1992.

Campen, Richard N. *Ohio—An Architectural Portrait*. Chagrin Falls, OH: West Summit Press, 1973.

Cassin-Scott, Jack. *The Illustrated Encyclopedia of Costume and Fashion from 1066 to the Present*. Revised and updated edition. London: StudioVista, 1994.

Chaddock, Robert E. *Ohio Before 1850: A Study of the Early Influence of Pennsylvania and Southern Populations In Ohio*. Originally published as Vol. XXXI, No. 2 of "Studies in History, Economics and Public Law" edited by the faculty of Political Science of Columbia University in 1908. New York: AMS Press, Inc., 1967.

Chartrand, Rene. *Uniforms and Equipment of the United States Forces in the War of 1812*. Youngstown, NY: Old Fort Niagara Association, Inc., 1992.

Clark, Ricky, George W. Knepper, and Ellice Ronsheim. *Quilts in Community: Ohio's Traditions, Nineteenth & Twentieth Century Quilts, Quiltmakers, and Traditions*. (Ohio Quilt Research Project) Nashville, TN: Rutledge Press, 1991.

Clayton, Andrew R. L. *Frontier Indiana*. [A History of the Trans-Appalachian Frontier Series] Bloomington: Indiana University Press, 1996.

Cole, Charles C., Jr. *Lion of the Forest: James B. Finley, Frontier-Reformer*. Lexington: University of Kentucky Press, 1994.

Contosta, David R. *Lancaster, Ohio, 1800–2000: Frontier Town to Edge City*. [Urban Life and Urban Landscape Series] Columbus: Ohio State University Press, 2000.

Cumming, Valerie. *Gloves*. [The Costume Accessories Series, Aileen Ribeiro, General Editor] London: B.T. Batsford Ltd, 1982. 1988.

Cunnington, C. Willett. *English Women's Clothing in the Nineteenth Century*. New York: Dover Publications, Inc., 1990.

Cunnington, C. Willett and Phyllis Cunnington. *The History of Underclothes*. First published, 1951; new edition includes revisions by A.D. Mansfield and Valerie Mansfield. London: Faber and Faber, 1981.

Davis, James E. *Frontier Illinois*. [A History of the Trans-Appalachian Frontier Series] Bloomington: Indiana University Press, 1998.

Deak, Gloria-Gilda. *American Views, Prospects and Vistas*. New York: The Viking Press and the New York Public Library, 1976.

Dwight, Margaret Van Horn. *A Journey to Ohio In 1810, as Recorded in the Journal of Margaret Van Horn Dwight*. Edited by Max Farrand. Introduction to the Bison Book Edition by Jay Gitlin. Reprint of 1913 edition by Yale University Press. Lincoln: University of Nebraska Press, 1991.

Earle, Alice Morse. *Two Centuries of Costume In America, Volume I*. Originally published by The Macmillan Company, 1903. Williamstown, MA: Corner House Publishers, 1974.

———. *Two Centuries of Costume In America, Volume II*. Originally published by The Macmillan Company. Williamstown, MA: Corner House Publishers, 1974.

Eggenberger, David. *Flags of the USA*. New York: Thomas Y. Crowell, 1964.

Ewing, Elizabeth. *Dress and Undress: A History of Women's Underwear*. New York: Drama Book Specialists, 1978.

———. *Everyday Dress, 1650–1900*. London: B.T. Batsford Ltd., 1984.

Fales, Martha Gandy. *Jewelry in America, 1600–1900*. Woodbridge, Suffolk: Antique Collectors' Club, Ltd., 1995.

Farrell, Jeremy. *Socks and Stockings*. [The Costume Accessories Series] London: B.T. Batsford Ltd., 1992.

Finke, Detmar H. and Marko Zlatich. "The Army Clothing Materials Estimate for 1804," *Military Collector and Historian*. Summer, 1994, Vol. XLIV, No. 2, 55–8.

Finley, James B. *Autobiography of Rev. James B. Finley, or Pioneer Life in the West*. Edited by W. P. Strickland. Cincinnati, OH: The Methodist Book Concern, 1856.

Fletcher, Marion. *Female Costume in the Nineteenth Century*. Melbourne: Oxford University Press., 1966.

Fogel, Robert William. *The Fourth Great Awakening and the Future of Egalitarianism*. Chicago: The University of Chicago Press, 2000.

Foster, Emily, ed. *The Ohio Frontier: An Anthology of Early Writings*. [The Ohio River Valley Series] Lexington: University Press of Kentucky, 1996.

Freshman, Phil, et al., eds. *An Elegant Art, Fashion & Fantasy in the Eighteenth Century*. Los Angeles County Museum of Art exhibition catalog. New York: Harry N. Abrams, Inc., 1983.

Fry, Mildred Covey. "Women on the Ohio Frontier: Marietta Area." *Ohio History*, Vol. 90, No. 1, Winter, 1981. 55–73.

Funcken, Liliane et Fred Funcken. *L'uniforme Et Les Armes Des Soldats Des Etats-Unis: Les Guerres D'independance, De Secession, Du Mexique. L'epopee Du Far-West*. Vol. 1, *L'infanterie et la marine.* Tournai, Belgium: Casterman, 1979.

Garrett, Elizabeth Donaghy. *The Arts of Independence: The DAR Museum Collection.* Washington, D.C.: National Society Daughters of the American Revolution, 1985.

———. *At Home: The American Family, 1750–1870.* New York: Harry N. Abrams, Inc., 1990.

Gehret, Ellen. *Rural Pennsylvania Clothing, Being a Study of the Wearing Apparel of the German and English Inhabitants, Both Men and Women Who Resided in Southeastern Pennsylvania in the Late Eighteenth and Early Nineteenth Century.* Includes patterns and sewing instructions. York, PA: G. Shumway Pub, Liberty Cap Books, 1976.

Gilgun, Beth. *Tidings from The 18th Century.* Texarkana, TX: Rebel Publishing Co., 1993.

Gorsline, Douglas. *What People Wore: 1,800 Illustrations from Ancient Times to the Early Twentieth Century.* [Originally published by Bonanza Books, NY in 1952 as *What People Wore: A Visual History of Dress from Ancient Times to Twentieth Century America*] New York: Dover Publications, Inc., 1994.

Gummere, Amelia Mott. *The Quaker: A Study in Costume.* First published in 1901. New York: Benjamin Blom, 1968.

"Hares, Bears, and Bobcats." Information supplied by the Ohio Division of Wildlife. Fairfield Soil and Water Conservation District, Lancaster, Ohio. *Fairfield Features,* Vol. 1, No. 3, August, 1999.

Heiser, Alta Harvey. *West to Ohio.* Yellow Springs, OH: The Antioch Press, 1954.

Hildreth, Samuel P. *The Hildreth Papers,* Vol. I and Vol. II. Dawes Collection. Marietta College Library, Marietta, Ohio.

Horsman, Reginald. "Hunger in a Land of Plenty, Marietta's Lean Years," *Timeline.* January–February, 2002, Vol. 19, No. 1, 20–31.

Houck, Carter. *The Quilt Encyclopedia Illustrated.* New York: Harry N. Abrams, Inc. (in association with The Museum of American Folk Art), 1991.

Hurchins, Catherine E., ed. *Everyday Life in the Early Republic.* Winterthur, DE: Henry Francis du Pont Winterthur Museum, 1994.

Hurt, R. Douglas. *The Ohio Frontier: Crucible of the Old Northwest, 1720–1830.* [A History of the Trans-Appalachian Frontier Series] Bloomington: Indiana University Press, 1996.

Hutslar, Donald A. *Log Construction in the Ohio Country, 1750–1850.* Athens: Ohio University Press, 1992.

Johnson, Barbara. *A Lady of Fashion: Barbara Johnson's Album of Styles and Fabrics.* Natalie Rothstein, ed. New York: Thomas and Hudson, 1987.

Journals of the Lewis and Clark Expedition, August 30, 1803–August 24, 1804. Vol. 2. Gary E. Moulton, editor. Lincoln: University of Nebraska Press, 1986.

Kidwell, Claudia. "Short Gowns," *Dress: The Journal of the Costume Society of America.* Vol. 4, 1978, 30–63.

Knepper, George W. *An Ohio Portrait.* Columbus: The Ohio Historical Society (for the Ohio American Revolution Bicentennial Advisory Commission), 1976.

———. *Ohio and Its People.* (2nd edition) Kent, OH: The Kent State University Press, 1989, 1997.

Kochan, James. *The United States Army 1783–1811.* Illustrated by David Rickman. [Men-at-Arms series #352] Oxford, UK: Osprey Publishing Limited, 2001.

Kunz, George Frederick. *Rings for the Finger.* Unabridged reproduction of the 1917 edition. New York: Dover Publications, 1973.

The Lady's Economical Assistant, or the Art of Cutting Out, and Making the Most Useful Articles of Wearing Apparel, Without Waste by a Lady. Originally published in London, 1808. Reprinted with additional preface, editorial notes, and illustrations. Springfield, OH: Kannik's Korner, 1998.

Larkin, Jack. *The Reshaping of Everyday Life, 1790–1840.* New York: Harper & Row, Publishers, 1988.

Laver, James. *The Concise History of Costume and Fashion.* New York: Harry N. Abrams, Inc., 1979.

Lester, Katherine Morris and Bess Viola Oerke. *Accessories of Dress.* Peoria, IL: The Manual Arts Press, 1940.

Lester, Katherine Morris, Rose Netzorg Kerr, and Dyann Gray. *Historic Costume: A Resume of Style and Fashion from Remote Times to the Nineteen-Seventies.* Seventh Edition, revised. Peoria, IL: Charles A. Bennett Co. Inc., 1977.

Loeffelbein, Robert L. *The United States Flagbook: Everything About Old Glory.* Jefferson, NC: McFarland and Company, Inc., 1996.

McClellan, Elisabeth. *Historic Dress in America, 1800–1870.* Philadelphia: G. W. Jacobs, 1910.

McCormick, Virginia. *New Englanders on the Ohio Frontier: Migration and Settlement of Worthington, Ohio.* Kent, OH: Kent State University Press, 1998.

McGaw, Judith A., ed. *Early American Technology: Making and Doing Things from the Colonial Era to 1850.* [Published for the Institute of Early American History and Culture, Williamsburg, Va.] Chapel Hill, NC: University of North Carolina Press, 1994.

McMurry, Elsie Frost. *American Dresses 1780–1900: Identification and Significance of 148 Extant Dresses.* Photographs by Mary Vivian White; Illustrations by Cathie Simpson. [book in CD format] Ithaca, NY: Cornell University, 2001.

Medert, Patricia Fife. *The Memoirs of a Pioneer Family.* [From the Samuel Williams Manuscript Collection, Ross County Historical Society Archives] Chillicothe, OH: Ross County Historical Society, 2000.

Miller, James M. *Genesis of Western Culture: The Upper Ohio Valley, 1800–1825.* Columbus: The Ohio State Archaeological and Historical Society, 1938.

Millett, Allan R. and Peter Maslowski. *For the Common Defense: A Military History of the United States of America.* New York: The Free Press, 1984.

Montgomery, Florence M. *Printed Textiles, English and American Cottons and Linens, 1700–1850.* A Winterthur Book. New York: The Viking Press, 1970.

Nelson, Henry Loomis. *Uniforms of the United States Army,* Vol. 1. Paintings by H. A. Ogden. New edition with new matter. New York: Sagamore Press, Inc., 1959.

Neumann, George C. *Swords and Blades of the American Revolution.* Harrisburg, PA: Stackpole Books, 1973.

Nunn, Joan. *Fashion in Costume, 1200–1980.* New York: Schocken Books, 1984.

Nylander, Jane C. *Our Own Snug Fireside: Images of the New England Home, 1760–1860.* New York: Alfred A. Knopf, Inc., 1993.

Peacock, John. *Costume 1066–1966.* London: Thames and Hudson, Ltd., 1986.

Picken, Mary Brooks. *A Dictionary of Costume and Fashion Historic and Modern.* Reprint of 1957 edition published by Funk & Wagnalls. Mineola, NY: Dover Publications, 1999.

Queen, Sally A. *Textiles for Colonial Clothing: A Workbook of Swatches and Information.* Arlington, VA: Q Graphics Production Company, 2000.

Rankin, Colonel Robert H. *Uniforms of the Army.* New York: G. P. Putnam's Sons, 1967.

Renick, Felix. "A Trip to the West," *American Pioneer.* Vol. 1, No. 2, February, 1842, 73–80.

Rexford, Nancy. *Women's Shoes in America, 1795–1930.* Kent, OH: Kent State University Press, 2000.

Ribeiro, Aileen. *The Art of Dress: Fashion in England and France, 1750–1820.* New Haven, CT: Yale University Press, 1995.

Riberio, Aileen and Valerie Cumming. *The Visual History of Costume*. London: B.T. Batsford Ltd., 1989.

Rohrbough, Malcolm J. *The Trans-Appalachian Frontier: People, Societies, and Institutions, 1775–1850*. New York: Oxford University Press, 1978.

Rodney, Thomas. *A Journey Through the West, Thomas Rodney's 1803 Journal from Delaware to the Mississippi Territory*. Edited by Dwight L. Smith and Ray Swick. Athens: Ohio University Press, 1997.

Rose, Clare. *Children's Clothes Since 1750*. London: B.T. Batsford, Ltd., 1989.

Ruby, Jennifer. *The Regency*. [Costume in Context Series] London: B.T. Batsford Ltd., 1989.

Saint-Pierre, Adrienne Elizabeth. "Clothing and Clothing Textiles in Ohio, Circa 1788 to 1835: A Study Based on Manuscript and Artifact Evidence." A thesis submitted in partial fulfillment of the requirements for the degree of Master of Humanities, Wright State University, 1988.

Sample, George. "Sketch of Western Settlements." *American Pioneer*. Vol.1, No. 4, April, 1842, 157–160.

Sanderson, George, Esq. *Early Settlement of Fairfield County Being the Substance of a Lecture Delivered Before the Lancaster Literary Institute with Additional Facts*. Lancaster, OH: Thomas Wetzler, 1851.

Sears, Alfred Byron. *Thomas Worthington: Father of Ohio Statehood*. Columbus: The Ohio State University Press, 1998.

Shep, R. L. *Federalist & Regency Costume*: 1790–1819. Mendocino, CA: R. L. Shep, 1998.

Sichel, Marion. *Costume Reference Vol. 5: Regency*. First American edition. Boston: Plays, Inc., 1978.

———. *History of Men's Costume*. London: Batsford Academic and Educational Ltd., 1984.

———. *History of Women's Costume*. London: Batsford Academic and Educational Ltd., 1984.

Stafford, Carleton L. and Robert Bishop. *America's Quilts and Coverlets*. New York: Weathervane Books, 1972.

Stone, Benjamin Franklin, Sr. *Reminiscence of an Early Pioneer in the Ohio Country: The Autobiography of Benjamin Franklin Stone, Sr., 1782–1873*. Marietta, OH: The Lemon Tree Press, 1992.

Sweet, William Warren. *Methodism In American History*. Revision of 1953 edition. Nashville, TN: Abingdon Press, 1961.

Tortora, Phyllis and Keith Eubank. *A Survey of Historic Costume: A History of Western Dress*. New York: Fairchild Publications, 1989.

Trobridge, Sophronia Howe. "Grandma Trobridge's Little Book." [Reprinted from a booklet originally published in 1875 by James Harper, Printer, Journal Office, Gallipolis, Ohio] in *The Tallow Light* [The Magazine of the Washington County Historical Society], Vol. 27, No. 3, Winter, 1996, 126–138.

Tunis, Edwin. *Frontier Living*. New York: Thomas Y. Crowell Company, 1961.

———. *The Young United States, 1783–1830: A Time of Change and Growth; A Time of Learning Democracy; A Time of New Ways of Living, Thinking and Doing*. New York: World Publishing Company, 1969.

Ulrich, Laurel Thatcher. *The Age of Homespun: Objects and Stories in the Creation of an American Myth*. New York: Alfred A. Knopf, 2001.

Valentine, Fawn. *West Virginia Quilts and Quiltmakers: Echoes from the Hills*. [With the West Virginia Heritage Quilt Search] Athens: Ohio University Press, 2000.

Walker, Joseph E., ed. "The Travel Notes of Joseph Gibbons, 1804." *Ohio History*. Vol. 92/Annual, 1983, pp. 96–146.

Waugh, Norah. *The Cut of Men's Clothes, 1600–1900*. New York: Theatre Arts Books, 1964.

———. *Corsets and Crinolines*. New York: Theatre Arts Books, 1969.

Weslager, C. A. *The Log Cabin In America: from Pioneer Days to the Present*. New Brunswick, NJ: Rutgers University Press, 1986.

Wharton, Anne Hollingsworth. *Social Life in the Early Republic*. Reprint of 1902 edition. Williamstown: Corner House Publishers, 1970.

Wilkinson, Frederick. *Antique Guns and Gun Collecting*. London: Hamlyn Publishing Group Limited, 1974.

Williams, John S. "Our Cabin; or, Life in the Woods," *The American Pioneer, a Monthly Periodical*. Logan Historical Society, Vol. II . Edited & published by John S. Williams. [Located in R.M. Stinson Collection of Marietta College Library] Cincinnati, OH: RP Books Printer, 1843.

Worrell, Estelle Ansley. *Children's Costume in America, 1607–1910*. New York: Charles Scribner's Sons, 1980.

The Workwoman's Guide by a Lady. A guide to 19th Century Decorative Arts, Fashion and Practical Crafts. [A facsimile reproduction of the original 1838 edition published in London by Simpkin, Marshall, and Co.] Guilford, CT: Opus Publications, 1986.

Wright, J. E. and Doris S. Corbett. *Pioneer Life in Western Pennsylvania*. Pittsburgh, PA: University of Pittsburgh Press, 1940.

Wright, Meredith. *Everyday Dress of Rural America, 1783–1800 with Instructions and Patterns*. Illustrated by Nancy Rexford. [Corrected and updated republication of *Put on Thy Beautiful Garments: Rural New England Clothing, 1783–1800* published by The Clothes Press, East Montpelier, Vermont, 1990] Mineola, NY: Dover Publications, Inc., 1992.

About the Authors and Illustrator

MARY K. INMAN and LOUISE F. PENCE are retired school librarians and media specialists who now specialize in frontier life and clothing, which they write about and also recreate for their living history presentations.

NORMA LU MEEHAN is a fashion illustrator who turned to creating historical-costume paper dolls in 1991.

She is author or illustrator of ten books, including four others from Texas Tech University Press: *The Fowler Family Gets Dressed,* in which Inman and Pence introduce the Fowlers; *Heroine of the Limberlost,* her paper doll biography of Gene Stratton Porter; and Collection by Design, a series on the Kent State University Museum costume collections.

▪▪■ Don't miss the beginning of the Fowler saga ■▪▪

The Fowler Family Gets Dressed
Frontier Paper Dolls of the Old Northwest Territory

It is autumn in the Ohio Country of 1790. The Fowlers are in a hurry to complete their farm chores. This afternoon they will walk three miles to attend a cornhusking and dance in their neighbors' new barn.

For audiences of all ages, this painstakingly detailed and illustrated work reflects the holdings of museums and historic sites as well as primary written sources in sharing a day in the lives of this frontier family and their Shawnee friends.

$10.95 paper

ISBN 0-89672-434-4

Back Cover

MAPS (not to scale)

The Northwest Territory, created from lands relinquished by seven of the original states, later became known as the Old Northwest Territory to distinguish it from the Pacific Northwest. In 1803, Ohio became the first state to be formed from the Northwest Territory. With the return of the Lewis and Clark Expedition in 1806 and the opening of the lands of the Louisiana Purchase, the American frontier continued moving westward. Indiana achieved statehood in 1816 and Illinois in 1818. The remaining states to be formed from this territory—Michigan, Wisconsin, and part of Minnesota—joined the Union as they filled with settlers. By 1820, Ohio was no longer considered frontier.

LOG CABIN

The Fowler family has replaced their original primitive log cabin with a true log house built of squared timbers. Chinking, the small pieces of wood and stone placed in the spacing between the logs, is held in securely with daubing or a mortar made of lime mixed with animal hair and straw. Since most log houses are one-and-a half stories, a full second floor is truly a luxury.

Fire is always a concern, but their stone chimney is much safer than ones made of logs and clay. The narrow stairwell, built into a corner near the chimney, leads to the second story with its two bedchambers. The wooden sash windows with glass panes let in light as well as fresh air. Mother is pleased with the puncheon floors made of split logs, an improvement over the dirt floors of many cabins. Although Father made the wooden shakes for the roof covering by hand, he was able to buy the iron nails to secure them. For the Fowler family, living in this log house is a dream come true.

Josiah

Josiah's shirt is based on the common cut of the time. The entire shirt is one length of linen fabric, with a hole cut for the neck and collar. Gussets and rectangular pieces of fabric reinforce the shirt and give room for movement. He tucks the long shirttails into his pantaloons as a kind of underwear. The sleeves are simply rectangles of fabric gathered onto the shirt body. All sewing is done by hand. As an officer, Josiah has his uniform tailored or sewn to meet specific guidelines.

Martha

Martha's linen shift, cross-stitched with her initials and number, is similar to Anna's. Based on woman's shift, about 1800–1815. Western Reserve Historical Society (85.12.9)

Washing of the linens includes scrubbing stains, and then stirring them in a large boiling kettle of water and lye soap. Sun drying them by laying the garments on bushes or shrubs ensures that the fabric will be continuously bleached.

George

White hand-woven linen shirt; reinforcing fabric strip is topstitched across top of shoulder line; neckcloth will cover one button at base of the collar; a second button at neck placket. Hand worked buttonhole also on each cuff. Based on man's shirt, about 1800–1850. Ohio Historical Society (H76441)

Tan colored knee breeches of homemade linen, with narrow front fall closing; buttons at knee. Based on man's wool breeches, about 1800–1825. Ohio Historical Society (H21610)

Thick hand knit cotton stockings; knee length.

Homemade moccasins are still practical footwear for everyday wear.

George

Martha

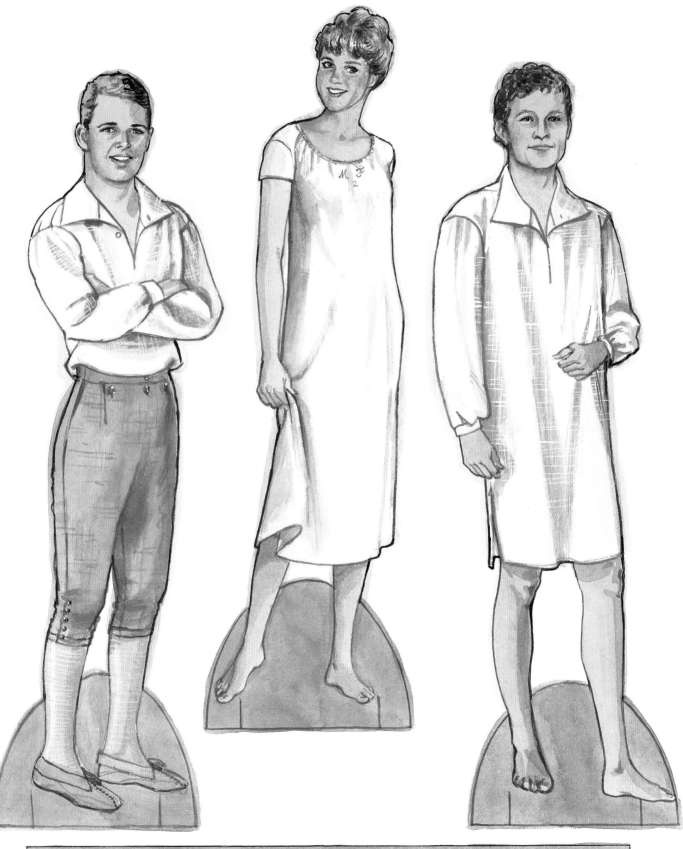

George

Josiah